DISTORTED ALLIANCE

Distorted Alliance

MARK SKELDING

ONION RIVER PRESS

To our country's true patriots, constitutionalists, and Christians, and to followers of other faiths, who sincerely respect and genuinely desire democracy.

CONTENTS

VIII –

PREFACE

I was born and raised in conservative eastern Pennsylvania, just a couple of miles from the Delaware River. My mother was a nurse and my stepfather was the CEO of a small health care business. My father was a salesman for a printing company until he became disabled from heart disease in his early forties. My stepmother was a stay-at-home mother of two sons from her previous marriage. My parents, all four of them, were middle class, racist, and very Republican, which I did not figure out until high school.

I started to become "political" when I was eleven years old and in sixth grade. I was elected president of my school's first student council. I gave a speech to the entire school body on the first Earth Day, sharing my thoughts on why it was so important to save our local creeks from certain known polluters. I wrote a petition on behalf of my classmates protesting the fact that every time we had a school assembly, it would be scheduled during our physical education ("gym") period. Most of us loved gym class and hated having it stolen from us. I gave the signature laden petition to my teacher, she called me to the front of the classroom, tore it up, and called me a rebel.

And then sometime during junior high school I started really questioning not just society, but human nature, itself.

It started when I realized how guilty I was feeling over how relatively rich my family was. Why us, and why not others? My worldview was taking shape. And at the core of that worldview were ideals I couldn't ignore ... wishing for fairness, equity, and a universal acceptance of equality, and hating power, wealth, privilege, selfishness, arrogance, and hypocrisy. No, I wasn't a Marxist. I didn't know anything about communism until later. My response to my disillusionment was to seek refuge in nature.

I'll share more of my life journey in my acknowledgements. But for now, I fast forward. My worldview is a synthesis of ecology, Christianity, critical social theory, holism, phenomenology, and constructivism. You'll see evidence of these as you read this book.

I began writing these commentaries in 2016. They've been a source of catharsis for me during the Donald Trump, "Make America Great Again" (MAGA) decade of 2015-25. As I write this, Trump is in the first months of his second term. No doubt, I will continue needing to somehow find solace.

I live in Vermont and although some of these commentaries have a Vermont-specific context, each is universally relevant. Whether you're a "liberal" or "conservative," I hope you will appreciate the sincerity and respect the whirlwind of disbelief and bewilderment that prompted them. And I'll wonder. Is it just me, or will you be left incredulous as well?

| 1 |

SAD! (2016)

Racists, bigots, xenophobes, supremacists, and national-ists are nothing new. They've been around and dividing our country since its beginning. What *is* new is a president (and his administration and Cabinet) who seems to empathize with all of them and openly sympathizes with one in particular, white nationalists.

White nationalists believe white Americans are losing their standing in society. They are especially irked that, in their minds, their demise is at the hands of non-whites and "non-Americans." Blacks are climbing America's career ladders, Hispanics are undercutting American workers and stealing their blue collar jobs, Jews are accumulating more than their fair share of America's wealth, and New Americans are taking over America's top white collar jobs.

Ironically, blacks, Hispanics, Jews, and New Americans are not the problem. They're simply participating in capitalism. The problem is capitalism, itself, and its inability to prevent unequal accumulation of wealth and truly provide equal economic opportunity for *all.*

Rather than hating and fighting to change the economic system that is failing them, white nationalists instead choose to hate and fight those who happen to be doing relatively well for now in that system ... just as they were when it was their turn to do so.

| 2 |

Hypocrisy (2016)

It would be ignorant and irresponsible to lump together the alt right, neo-Nazis, Republicans, white nationalists, Libertarians, white supremacists, the Tea Party, and others of the conservative right as one and the same. However, what they have in common is a bit alarming.

For one, they're all parties of fear and anger. Each fears losing what they believe gives them power and standing in society, and they're angry at groups who they perceive are the beneficiaries of their loss. Consequently, their political bottom lines are the same ... protecting their self-interests over the interests of others. Trump and his administration, sycophants, and surrogates fit this bill perfectly. They'll argue they're out for what's best for our country but it's difficult to find anything they're proposing and fighting for that doesn't ultimately boil down to selfish gain, self-protection, self-preservation, and self-centeredness.

There's a second, rather contradictory commonality among right wing groups. Their subscribers generally claim to belong to the Christian church. If so, then what's with all the fear and hate, and why aren't they humbly viewing others above themselves and putting others' needs ahead of their own?

| 3 |

True Patriots (2017)

The growing number of professional athletes and others kneeling during our national anthem is causing outrage. Those offended say these people are unpatriotic and their actions are a slap in the face to our men and women who defend our flag. Those who side with the protesters say they are simply exercising their First Amendment right to free speech. Who's correct?

The answer comes down to which defines our country… our flag, or our Constitution?

Unlike the flag, the Constitution literally defines America. And embedded in that definition is the guaranteed right of every American to freely and without fear of reprisal express their beliefs and concerns. It makes sense, then, that our true patriots are those who live by and defend our Constitution. By honoring our Constitution they honor our country.

And our flag? It's no small hypocrisy that some of our most ardent defenders of allegiance to our flag are divisive white nationalists who pay greater homage to the Confederate flag than the U. S. flag, and states' rights advocates who essentially want less national unity, not more. These people are quick to cry out to the protesters, "Love it (the *United* States) or leave it!" Again, the hypocrisy is astonishing. Their fake allegiance to our flag, frustration with free speech, and disdain for the protesters clearly reveal they don't love our country.

And finally, shame on those who are using our military and veterans as cover to hide the real reason they hate those who are kneeling. Our military does not defend our flag. The image of our troops encircling every flagpole in our country 24/7 is comical. Our military defends our country, which means they defend our Constitution. And that means they are defending our right to kneel during the national anthem.

| 4 |

American Exceptionalism?
(2017)

During his campaign, Donald Trump routinely lied to voters, deceived his supporters, bullied his opponents, threatened and demeaned multiple segments of our population, and made grandiose promises he had no idea how he would actually fulfill or at what cost.

Regardless, fourteen million Americans voted for him in the 2016 primary election.

By the time the presidential election rolled around we knew him to be a pathological liar, hypocrite, narcissist, bully, misogynist, and sexual assaulter. We had evidence suggesting he's a white nationalist, racist, and bigot.

Regardless, nearly sixty three million Americans elected him to be our president.

And what's even more astonishing is after two years of witnessing these traits and behaviors on a nearly daily basis, close to 40% of Americans and the GOP majority continue to stand by him.

He said Washington, D.C. was a swamp that needed draining yet some of those he's backfilled with are under federal investigation and being indicted. He says protesters are unpatriotic yet it is he who wants to do away with freedom of press and loathes the fact that the Executive Branch doesn't have more power to dictate. He belittled Obama's use of executive orders saying he used them because he couldn't get anything done legislatively. What was *his* number of executive orders up to before finally being able to sign his first piece of legislation?

He calls cable and network news "fake news" yet his tweets, rally speeches, and press conferences are rife with lies and unsubstantiated claims. His recent tweet accusing cable news of being fake news has put international reporters' lives in danger. Foreign dictators are now using his claim that American news is fake as a way to sow doubt among their people over any bad press they receive coming from the U.S. He criticizes reporters' use of anonymous sources yet hides behind them himself when his lies are exposed. He says he's all about "Made in America" and "Buy American, Hire American" yet his wealth has come from outsourcing and offshore bank accounts. He taunted Clinton aides for pleading the fifth yet encouraged his own people to do the same.

He criticized Obama for going on golf outings yet in less than a year golfed more and spent more on travel at taxpayer expense than Obama did in eight years. He wants our taxes to pay for increased military spending and a border wall yet he's a tax evader. He tried to shame Obama for not following through on his red line with Syria but in the span of just a couple of weeks drew several new red lines with North Korea and continues to draw more. He says he's all about protecting Americans and America's interests yet disparages our allies and taunts our adversaries. He mocked John McCain for getting captured in Vietnam yet he avoided military service.

He cries foul when he's personally attacked yet look at his tweets. He said, "I love *all* Americans." Again, look at his tweets.

These examples are barely the tip of the iceberg of Trump's hypocrisy and lies. And every time I try to conclude this commentary more becomes available. Most recently, his support of Roy Moore, taunting North Korea over whose nuclear button is bigger, and his racist comment about "s**thole(house)" countries. As well, there's his refusal to call out Putin, impose Congress mandated sanctions on Russia, admit Russian meddling in our election, and aggressively defend Americans by going after Russian hackers. Need I mention ever-growing suspicion over his financial practices?

Regardless, he remains our president because enough Americans are willing to look the other way and excuse him. So what's this claim we hear about American exceptionalism?

| 5 |

Repeal and E'race' (2017)

Those of us following the right wing's desperate attempts to repeal and replace the Affordable Care Act (ACA) have seen through their quest from the start. Why would Republicans and Libertarians be so vindictive toward someone who sincerely wanted to help as many Americans as possible, had the courage to take on an industry that's making obscene profits at the expense of Americans, and was smart enough to figure out how to do both? And, why else would they want so desperately to completely do away with ACA rather than simply fix those parts of it that are not working as effectively as they could?

The answer couldn't be more obvious, and Trump's desperate executive order on health care he signed on October 12, 2017 confirms it. They cannot stand the fact that a black man, a first time black president and a Democrat no less, was the one finally to have the compassion, courage, and "IQ" to do what's right when it comes to health care in this country.

The right wants us to believe this isn't racism, and their true concern is for our country. They say ACA is one more step toward the U.S. becoming socialist and anyone who doesn't trust that the free market will take care of the problem is a fool.

If free market competition had worked with the healthcare industry in the first place we wouldn't be in this position. And, if allegiance to capitalism and hatred of socialism are the right's true motivators, why aren't they attacking, with the same virulence, the many social programs and "anti-free market" policies put in place by our other presidents?

The right wing's repeal and replace Obama Care effort is a desperate attempt to save face. They were beaten to the punch by the Democrats and a black president and that sticks in their craw. And their underlying worship of an economic policy that has never worked because human greed won't allow it to is proving rigid and foolish. But they cling to it regardless because what else can they do? It's what defines them.

| 6 |

Conservatives Really Aren't (2017)

Conservatives are known as the party of fiscal responsibility and frugality. But they're not just about spending less, saving more, reducing our budget deficit, and managing the federal budget responsibly. What they want to "conserve" extends broader, deeper, and is more personal to them than that.

"Conserve" is in quotation marks because it's not really conservation that underlies what the right is all about. It's preservation. To conserve means to limit the use of something so that it will last, to use wisely and sparingly, or to set aside and protect something for prosperity or later use. To preserve means to keep as is, to save something in its original or present form, to essentially embalm.

Fighting to protect family and Christian values isn't an attempt to conserve them, it's an effort to preserve them.

Attempting to regain and maintain a white majority in America by way of ethnic travel bans, bigoted immigration laws, and border walls is an act of preservation, not conservation.

Legislating against and verbally and physically assaulting members of the LGBT community isn't an attempt to conserve heterosexuality and a particular definition of marriage. It's an effort to institutionalize them.

Steadfast support of free market capitalism combined with hatred of anything that smacks of socialism is an attempt to preserve one particular economic system at the expense of others.

Fighting against government overreach and intrusion into our personal lives isn't fighting to conserve a healthy balance between personal sovereignty and social responsibility. It's about preserving individual sovereignty, period.

Cutting support for government assistance programs under the guise of reducing the federal budget and ending government perpetuation of laziness and voluntary unemployment isn't an act of conservation. The right supports this because they believe a lower deficit will help *preserve* our standing in the global economy and doing away with public assistance programs helps *preserve* the image of capitalism. Having hundreds of thousands of citizens on government support because they can't find work and are living in poverty exposes the fact that the "promise" of capitalism is a myth.

Given that their platform is built on their faith in free market economics, the right certainly can't have that.

And here's a recent example that really helps distinguish preservation from conservation. Committing to vote yes on a tax reform bill you haven't read, and is in fact still being written and amended, just so you can "get a legislative win," be able to tell your constituents you got something done, and hopefully not get voted out of office is the epitome of being a preservationist.

All of this raises a question worth reflecting on and a point worth arguing. When you boil these examples down, isn't the bottom line in all of them self-preservation of some kind, whether it's one's personal security, power, wealth, status, identity, or world view?

Worth arguing is the fact that preservation is antithetical to how the universe works. Nothing is static. Everything is in a perpetual state of evolution, and transformation and extinction are natural processes. Change happens. It always has, and will, and to not embrace it is, well … SAD.

| 7 |

Separating Religion and Politics? (2018)

Separation of church and state is fundamental to democracy. But separation of church and state isn't the same as separating our religion (which, for Americans, is primarily Christian) from our politics. Yet it seems we're becoming a nation who sees no difference between the two.

Supporters of Republican Senatorial candidate Roy Moore are a striking example of this. Their attempt late last year to elect him to represent their version of Christianity, family values, and character while excusing him for alleged behavior contrary to Christian doctrine is ... actually, it's hard to find words for what it is.

What about these next examples? Are they evidence of how insidious compartmentalizing our spirituality from our words and actions has become?

First is an unbending allegiance to the Second Amendment and relentless opposition to gun control. The Second Amendment is essentially a government ("Caeser") decree.

It was written by flawed and fallible men during a unique context in our nation's history and for more than two hundred years has been variably interpreted by state and federal courts. Instead, wouldn't honoring the Sixth Commandment (never committing murder) *and* doing everything in our control to help keep others from being able to commit murder be more in line with our nation's professed faith?

A second example is free market competition and trickle down economics. The advantaged climb to the top and accumulate greater and greater proportions of our wealth but sufficient voluntary redistribution of that wealth (described in various ways throughout the Bible) clearly isn't happening. Isn't free market economics more reflective of Darwinian survival of the fittest and evolution of species than of Christianity?

Free market competition and health care fits this pattern, too. Prior to the Affordable Care Act we especially saw this. Leaving health care in the hands of for-profits is survival of the fittest at its worst. Those who are the "fittest" financially can afford to pay steadily rising health care costs while those who are less "fit" either go untreated or into crippling debt. Wouldn't supporting universal health care be more in line with Christian compassion?

Two especially glaring examples of this disconnect are nationalism and patriotism. The Bible clearly reveals that there are no geo-political boundaries or national identity to the Church. People of one nation are no better or worse than those of other nations, and we're to indiscriminately love our neighbors even to the point of loving our enemies.

Regarding patriotism, Christians know they're not to be idolatrous or worship false gods.

Our current push for exclusionary immigration laws is contradictory, as well. Some argue such laws are needed for our safety, but our faith tells us that with belief in God we've nothing to fear. Others argue these laws are needed because immigrants are taking Americans' jobs, yet the Bible promises that God will provide and we shall not want. A third argument is essentially that America is for Americans. Wouldn't our nation be truer to our professed faith if we welcomed all people into the fold, humbly putting them above ourselves and their needs ahead of our own?

Examples like these abound, and here's one more ... deregulation. Rescinding regulatory safeguards and freeing corporations to profit at the expense of human health and safety is hardly caring for others as we would have others care for us. And how does doing away with environmental regulations, gutting the Environmental Protection Agency, and giving industry a free pass to exploit our resources and degrade the environment square with our biblical charge of stewardship?

The hypocrisy we witnessed coming out of Alabama last fall was shocking. Its dismissal in the White House and lukewarm condemnation from congressional lawmakers were even more so. And just when we think it can't get any worse, Tony Perkins, president of Family Research Council (a pro-life, evangelical Christian organization) publicly excuses Donald Trump for his pre-presidency adultery in exchange for him being a conservative political force, despite the fact Trump continuously disregards at least four other commandments. And now we have the porn star and Play-boy playmate scandals routinely being dismissed by conservatives, as well. But maybe being jolted by hypocrisy such as this is a good thing given how numb we've become to our slow but steady normalization of separating our religion from our politics.

Our political views are a direct reflection of our underlying character and regard for others. They are also an extension of our religious beliefs. It's disingenous to argue that separation of religion and politics is possible. If it were, then what's the point of religion?

| 8 |

Are Conservatives America's True Patriots? (2018)

Conservatives argue they are America's true patriots. Are they right? First, a look at patriotism.

Patriotism is often defined as loyalty to one's country. But a country is simply a geographically defined area with politically determined borders. Within those borders lives a nation, the *collective peoples* who inhabit that country. Nations exist, and persist, only by adhering to and allowing themselves to be governed by the economic, social, and political structures that bind them together. For Americans, that includes things like the Constitution, Bill of Rights, laws, a justice system separate from the Executive Branch, and an Executive Branch that is not above the law.

Boil that down and we see patriotism is not loyalty to one's country. It's loyalty to one's nation, which in turn means allegiance first and foremost to one's fellow citizens.

For without people there are no institutions, no nation, and no country.

Though he says he's loyal to the American people, Donald Trump, a Republican, is not. He steals money from Americans through tax evasion and off-shore bank accounts. He robs Americans of work by outsourcing jobs overseas. He refuses to seriously do anything about Russian interference in our elections, has destroyed relations with our allies, and threatens our national security through bullying and isolationism. He undermines the Constitution, degrades the office of President, disparages our justice system in front of the world, and continually makes a mockery of the American electorate. Trump is clearly no patriot.

The Republican National Committee and Republican House and Senate are no better. Whether cowardice or calculated, their silent support of Trump while he continues his unpatriotic tirade suggests they are no patriots either.

Given the behavior of these officials, *chosen by conservative voters to represent and lead them*, it's a fair question to ask. Are conservatives as patriotic as they say they are? Are the American people truly their bottom line? Let's look.

Consider their zeal for cutting taxes and public assistance programs. Conservatives argue that we should be entitled to the money we earn. The more we're allowed to keep, the more we'll invest in stimulating the economy, creating jobs, and giving to charity for those in need. By reducing taxes, we eliminate the need for costly social programs. Unfortunately, it's well documented that trickle-down economics is a myth and charitable donations don't go far enough. Cutting taxes … altruistic patriotism or selfish greed?

What about exclusionary immigration policies? Most of us have ancestors who immigrated to this country and it was they who built this nation. Despite that, conservatives argue that drastically limiting (or eliminating) the number of foreigners who get to live and work in this country will preserve jobs for Americans. But our own history has proven the morality and pragmatism of welcoming immigrants. And ecology and economics confirm that the key to sustainability is diversity. One doesn't have to look any further than American technology and health care industries to see that people of diverse cultures are moving this nation forward. So which is ultimately for the greater good of the American people, progress or preservation?

A third example is their fervor for government deregulation. They argue that corporations and businesses would be more productive and profitable if they weren't being regulated to death by the federal government. Deregulation would free them to reinvest profits toward stimulating the economy and creating more jobs. But our growing gap between rich and poor, as well as business leaders, themselves, admitting (November, 2017 Wall Street Journal CEO Council meeting) they would not reinvest their gains from Trump's tax cuts prove this argument flawed. Regulation, on the other hand, protects against monopolies, helps protect the health and safety of workers, consumers, and the environment, creates jobs required to carry out regulatory processes, and stimulates innovation in figuring out how to comply with regulations and thrive at the same time. Again, which of the two puts the American people's well-being first?

Other examples of conservative principles worth analyzing through the lens of patriotism include opposition to equal access health care, opposition to gun control and abortion, opposition to protesting during the national anthem (i.e., right to free speech), advocacy for greater states' rights, worship of capitalism (which by default means a class system), and Libertarian allegiance to individual sovereignty. A close look may likely reveal they and their kind are their bottom line (see "Conservatives Really Aren't," <u>VTDigger.org/commentary</u>, Dec. 7, 2017), not the American people.

Given all we've witnessed since Trump made his infamous descent on his golden escalator, we are justified in not only questioning the conservative party's claim they're the party of Christian faith and family values (see "Separating Religion and Politics," <u>VTDigger.org/commentary</u>, April 9, 2018), but also whether they're America's true patriots.

| 9 |

Socialist Conservatives?
(2018)

In past commentaries I've questioned conservatives' claims that they are the party of patriotism, conservatism, and Christian family values. Their steadfast lack of outrage toward Trump and their elected leaders who continue to aid and abet him just furthers my suspicion. Watch how House Oversight Committee Republicans represented conservatives during the Michael Cohen hearing and, well, enough said.

I also question just how sincere conservatives are when it comes to capitalism. This is especially timely given Trump's con *du jour* of trying to brainwash his supporters into believing "liberals" are dangerous socialists who need to be feared and hated. Look at the irony here.

Workers are struggling to make ends meet. Consequently, many are advocating for living wage legislation. In the meantime, some are accepting government help and are grateful for the financial assistance. Is it only working class liberals advocating for the government to get involved in setting wages? Are working class conservatives protesting *en masse* over the living wage movement? And are they publicly denouncing and returning all public assistance they receive? No.

Many working class Americans are angry that employers, in keeping with the capitalist principle that competition drives down cost, are hiring people, minorities in particular, willing to work for minimum wage or less. Consequently, they want legislation that not only opposes hiring immigrants but immigration itself. As well, they cry foul when company executives outsource jobs overseas, a perfectly capitalist (albeit, unpatriotic), free market thing to do.

The "Buy American, Hire American" slogan and the notion of only doing business in America have become popular with many working class Americans, particularly conservatives. But economic isolation is completely contrary to the capitalist principle of free market competition. So, too, are import tariffs, quotas, and other government job protection and price control measures.

When Americans feel they're getting price gouged at the gas pump, pharmacy, or wherever because either the retailer has a monopoly on the product or retailers of that product are conspiring to fix prices, again, conservatives have no problem with the government intervening to stop selfish capitalists.

When a company is approaching bankruptcy and the government provides a bailout, it's rare we see employee outrage over their jobs being spared. Did conservative auto workers march in protest when their employer was bailed out? No. And haven't they historically relied on their union leaders to negotiate government protections on their behalf? Yes.

No doubt there are other similar examples of their hypocrisy. Conservatives claim they are anti-tax, anti-big government, "free market" capitalists (well, except when it comes to the military, infrastructure, transportation safety, law enforcement, food and drug safety, border security, immigration, etc., etc., etc.). Yet when their personal financial well-being is threatened we see something completely different. They willingly participate in an economy that, go figure, looks more like socialism than capitalism.

Working class conservatives are a large segment of Donald Trump's base. They support him because they believe he reflects their character, shares their values, and will represent them accordingly. Ironically, they also believe that because he's a businessman he will know how to protect their paychecks. Sadly, he's deceived them on that one. He's bent on providing tax breaks for entrepreneurs. Those tax breaks widen the gap between rich and poor and further fuel a survival of the fittest economy. They ensure a struggling, perhaps desperate class of workers willing to work for cheap but who, in turn, will need financial assistance. But public assistance programs are funded with tax money. If entrepreneurs pay little to no taxes, where's that needed funding going to come from?

Perhaps conservatism isn't all it's cracked up to be for the working class. And as for Trump's latest deceit, are Democrats for socialism, or are they simply for saving capitalism from itself?

| 10 |

Constitutionalists, Please Step Up (2019)

It's probably safe to say most Americans appreciate our constitution, or at least understand and respect its importance. But evidence suggests that conservatives, particularly since the unleashing of Trump, may not be the constitutionalists they claim.

For starters, how in good conscience can they continue to align themselves with Trump? His reckless disregard for the constitution and its principles are no secret. His own words and actions to that effect are well documented.

He wants to ban Muslims, he ignores emoluments laws, and he interferes with justice department investigations. He tries to bypass Congress on appropriations and war powers, he wants to limit freedom of speech and means of protest, he encourages hatred toward the press, and he wants to abolish judges. He delays nominating cabinet secretaries for congressional confirmation so he can simply install "acting" sycophants willing to do his autocratic bidding, legal or not.

And now both he and his puppet attorney general, William Barr, are essentially saying, "No! Make me!" to congressional oversight requests.

If conservatives worship the constitution as they claim, where is their outrage? Why are they not withdrawing their support for Trump and publicly denouncing him and their GOP House and Senate members who are aiding and abetting his self-serving assault on our constitution?

This, alone, justifies questioning whether conservatives are truly loyal to the constitution. There are other examples, of course.

Rather than spewing hatred toward the FBI and Special Counsel for exposing the truth and trying to hold Trump and his associates accountable for their crimes, wouldn't true constitutionalists be basking in the fact that our justice department is working as intended?

Is assaulting BBC camera persons while screaming, "CNN sucks!" the way constitutionalists now express their belief in the sanctity of a free press?

Instead of attacking protesters, wouldn't respecting their right to freedom of speech show true adherence to the constitution (and by default, true patriotism)?

Doesn't cheering on efforts clearly designed to make it more difficult for the poor and New Americans to participate in elections show disregard for the constitutional principles of equality and popular sovereignty?

And by applauding and encouraging Trump when he attempts to take power away from Congress and give it to himself, aren't conservatives undermining the constitutional principles of separation of powers and checks and balances?

This is my fifth in a series of commentaries questioning the sincerity of today's conservatives. The first four focused on the illusion that they are the party of conservatism, Christianity, patriotism, and capitalism.

Some argue I overgeneralize in these commentaries. It's true, there are conservatives who don't fit this bill. But where are they? Their silent complicity and head-in-the-sand approach to all things Trump isn't helping discredit the notion that apparently they really are all hypocrites.

Some question what I have against conservatives. It's not them, it's their hypocrisy. They claim with indignation they are our country's models of constitutionalism, conservatism, patriotism, capitalism, and Christianity. In all five cases there's damning evidence to the contrary.

Ironically, their hypocrisy is inherent. What underlies all five of these, theoretically even capitalism, is our "better angel" sense of how important it is for us to do for others, not just ourselves and our families. And that is the dilemma for conservatives. Dissect conservative ideals, policies, or party platforms down to their core essence and what you find is that self-interest trumps all. Hostility toward immigration, gun laws, equal access health care, tax supported government assistance, and the rest all boil down to some form of self-gain at the expense of others.

I'm self-centered, too. But what I'm not is out there self-righteously proclaiming and venomously defending allegiance to things I don't come even close to practicing.

| 11 |

Make America Good
(2020)

Critics of liberals and progressives know they are fake branding both parties, yet they persist. It leaves you wondering whether they're doing it for nefarious purposes.

The term "liberal" comes from the Latin word *liber*, which means free. We hear the word commonly used in phrases such as liberal helpings of food, liberal interpretations of the law, and liberal donations to charity. Break them down and we see that liberal refers to a generous amount or array that's shared freely. In short, it's about generosity, sharing, and giving.

Liberals are true to their title. Sharing wealth through government assistance programs is not out of control spending or giving lavish handouts as critics of liberals would have you believe. Actually, it's thoughtful spending in both senses of the word thoughtful. It is generosity out of a sense of compassion for those inevitably left behind in a capitalist society. It's also sharing with fellow Americans to help free them from poverty so they, in turn, can contribute back to our economy.

Generosity and concern for our neighbors sounds like something right out of the Bible doesn't it? It looks a lot like genuine patriotism, too.

As for progressives, during the 2016 Democratic primary, Hillary Clinton stated that like Bernie Sanders, she is a progressive because she believes in progress and the good that comes from it. That's true of progressives but there's more to it than that. Progressives understand systems and how they work. Consequently, they recognize that progress is more than just moving forward. Progress is ongoing change within a system; change that doesn't simply maintain (conserve/preserve) but actually sustains the system. And that can only happen if all the diverse parts of the system are coevolving, continuously shaping and reshaping one another. Simply put, progress is evolution, and evolution involves both transformation and extinction.

This understanding is at the root of why progressives value human diversity, recognize that all things are interdependent, and accept that "extinction" of things as we know them (the coal industry, for example) is natural.

Sharing wealth by allocating money toward progress-minded initiatives (renewable energy sources, for example) and making accessible to everyone the education required for those initiatives to succeed and progress to occur isn't indulgent, irresponsible, or wasteful spending as critics of progressives would have you believe. It's a caring attempt to increase employment opportunities, particularly for those whose line of work is going "extinct," and help sustain our country's economy.

Doesn't that sound a lot like religious compassion and true patriotism, too?

Progressives and liberals genuinely care about America and not just themselves, their families, their finances, and their kind. They sincerely want to help make America good.

| 12 |

Unmasking the Right (2020)

Despite choosing Donald Trump to be their shining example on the hill, conservatives insist they are the party of Christian family values and true American patriotism. They are also the party leading the protest against wearing face masks during this deadly COVID-19 pandemic.

For sure, the primary reason many are not wearing masks fits one of their conservative party values. Individual freedoms are paramount and an overreaching government is an enemy to be defied and dismantled. But how well does not wearing a mask square with being a Christian and a patriot? First, we'll review some facts about this coronavirus.

We are being encouraged to wear masks to protect ourselves from others *and others from ourselves*. This virus spreads by way of the aerosol that comes from our noses and mouths. That aerosol is expelled not just through sneezing and coughing, but simply by talking and breathing. Masks help block the aerosol from entering our noses and mouths.

People who are infected with the virus spread it even if they aren't feeling sick or showing signs of being infected. If we get the disease and recover we can still get it again. And finally, there are highly vulnerable groups within our population, the elderly and those with compromised immune systems, for example, who have a high probability of dying if they contract this disease.

Conservatives who claim they are Christian, it can be assumed, read the Bible and adhere to its teaching. Is there anything in the Bible that applies to one's choice to not wear a mask during a pandemic?

One of the Ten Commandments is "Thou shalt not kill." We know there's no way of knowing whether we, or anyone we come into contact with, is infected unless we get tested for the virus. But even if we get tested, because the virus spreads so easily and rapidly we could contract it literally minutes after testing negative. And even if we are asymptomatic we could still have the virus and be spreading it. So what if, knowing all of this, we still choose to not wear a mask, infect someone, and they die? We knowingly, willingly, and willfully engaged in behavior we knew would likely cost someone their life.

Christians believe it is right to treat others as you want to be treated. If those not wearing masks believe they are in accordance with this teaching, are they saying they don't want others to guard against giving them the virus?

Being humble, selfless, and putting others first are at the core of Jesus's teachings. If others' needs are to not get sick and die, and we choose to not wear a mask, are we being humble and putting others before ourselves?

What about this admonition from the Bible? Give to Caesar (government) what is Caesar's and to God what is God's. In most states, having to wear a mask isn't even a local or state mandate. It's simply a guideline officials are imploring people to follow. Of the Christian ways we've looked at, aside from not killing someone you would think this one would be an easy one to put into practice.

No doubt readers could add many more examples like these to the list. But to allow for balance, are there biblical passages that justify not wearing a mask during a novel coronavirus pandemic?

As for patriotism, being patriotic means loving, protecting, and being loyal to the nation to which you belong. A nation is the collective people who live within the geo-political boundaries of a given country. In other words, being patriotic means loving, protecting, and being loyal to, in our case, our fellow Americans. If we choose to not wear a mask during a pandemic, are we loving and protecting our fellow countrymen and countrywomen?

It was a great unmasking of conservatives in 2016 when they chose to compromise all of their values and elect Donald Trump in hopes he would do away with Roe v. Wade and stop the "slaughter of innocents." Odd, considering they're unwilling to do anything to stop the massacre of innocents through gun violence. And now they're further unmasking themselves by venomously defending an action that's leading to the deaths of even more innocents.

| 13 |

Dichotomy, Hypocrisy, and Humility (2023)

"**B**ut please don't call it patriotism. Don't pretend it's about freedom. Because real patriots serve and sacrifice for all - whether they agree with them or not." Governor Phil Scott stated this during his November 17, 2020 Covid-19 Update press conference covered by WCAX. I'll come back to his quote, but first ...

There are basic dichotomies we all wrestle with. For example, are there absolutes or is everything relative? Can absolutes be relative? Maybe it's relativity that's absolute.

At some point in our lives we align ourselves with the sides of these dichotomies we believe are prevailing truths. Those "truths" shape our world view and guide how we live our lives ... and of course our politics.

Absolutism versus relativism is one dichotomy. Others include an individual's rights vs. the rights of others, competition vs. cooperation, independence vs. interdependence, selfishness vs. selflessness, and humility vs. arrogance and narcissism.

Republicans and Democrats generally find themselves on opposite sides of each of these dichotomies. It makes sense, since left and right are opposites

Republicans generally fall on the sides of absolutes, competition, independence, and individual sovereignty and hands-off government. Democrats typically espouse relativism, cooperation, interdependence, and equal rights and the necessity of government. Here are quick examples for both.

Republicans support the concept of capitalism. They believe that every individual has an equal opportunity to achieve prosperity if they are willing to compete with one another in an economy free of "excessive" government interference. They maintain it's as simple as that.

Democrats, on the other hand, argue that it's not that black or white. They believe systemic inequities exist within capitalism that give some a privileged head start while prohibiting others from ever being able to truly compete. Opportunity to prosper is relative, especially in an economy that is not free but instead completely dependent on a highly regulated global (*inter*dependent) market.

In these two examples we clearly see self vs. other, individual vs. society, government is bad vs. government is good, competition vs. cooperation, independence vs. interdependence, and absolutes exist vs. everything is relative.

So back to Governor Scott's quote and the title of this commentary.

Conservatives, by and large, claim to be patriots and Christians (or "Christian" nationalists*) and that their words, actions, and deeds are driven by their allegiance to the Constitution of the United States, democracy, the Bible, and the sovereignty of God. Regarding patriotism, Governor Scott couldn't have said it any better. "... real patriots serve and sacrifice for all ..." As for Christianity, the key tenets of the faith are humility and selflessness (putting others before self).

If we look at each dichotomy it appears there's a contradiction between who conservatives say they are versus how they act? The party, in general, fights to ensure that individuals' freedoms aren't compromised by the rights of others or for the good of society (take, for example, their stand against gun control and government-led vaccination programs). They defend competition, despite knowing it naturally keeps others down (somebody has to lose). They argue for less government, knowing a) it will mean less help for others in need (who will always be among us) and b) that trickle-down economics and charity don't fill that need. They stand by capitalism and a person's right to accumulate wealth (storing up vs. giving away; one person's gain is another's loss). And, they believe in independence ("I alone...") and individual sovereignty despite the fact that every aspect of their lives is dependent on others.

Clearly the conservative platform is steeped in self. Given who their party's current front runner for president is, that couldn't be more blatant. So even though patriotism and Christianity are all about prioritizing others over self, most conservatives contend they're patriots and Christians.

And finally, narcissism. It is principally Republicans rabidly denouncing woke, a call for us to "... be aware of and actively attentive to important societal facts and issues (especially issues of racial and social injustice) ..." (Merriam-Webster definition). They are afraid of having America, and consequently themselves, exposed and our country's "exceptionalism" questioned. Their crusade is a narcissistic one. A narcissist is someone who is unable to recognize, admit, and accept their faults and mistakes. They are unable to own up to the fact that they, like all of us, have an ugly side. They are void of humility.

America's patriots recognize and accept that their *nation* (government *and* citizenry) isn't perfect yet humbly serve and sacrifice for her. Christians humbly recognize and accept that humans are imperfect, that they have an ugly side. And woke is simply a call for us as a *nation* to humbly assess equity in our society rather than be arrogant and defensive about it.

So if conservatives are patriots and Christians, how can there be such a dichotomy between who they say they are and who they actually are?

If we take an honest look at what nationalism is and compare it to the fundamental message of Christianity it's hard to argue the two aren't completely contradictory. The term "Christian nationalist" is an oxymoron.

| 14 |

Deep State, Indeed (2024)

S ince 2015, the Republican Party has been rebranding it-self, starting with Trump Republicans, then Party of Trump, MAGA, and now Christian Nationalists. This latest iteration is spearheaded by conservative groups including the New Apostolic Reformation, Turning Point USA, the Federalist Society, the Conservative Political Action Conference, the Center for Renewing America, The Heritage Foundation, the Freedom Caucus, and the Republican National Committee.

One of those groups, The Heritage Foundation (THF), has released a manifesto titled Project 2025: Presidential Transition Project, which is an excellent reveal of who these conservatives are and what they actually stand for.

In the agenda THF has laid out for our next conservative president, we see everything from mass deportation and punishing political opponents to dismantling the Constitution and eliminating regulatory and rights-protecting agencies, including the Department of Education. In short, it's an attempt to reverse any policy or legislation that has sustained democracy, equality, equal rights, equal opportunity, sharing of wealth, and regulations intended to protect *every* American.

Said differently, it's an all out effort to reinstitutionalize overt privilege and supremacy for *certain* Americans. Most telling of this fact is their disdain for anything supporting diversity, equity, and inclusion (DEI). Their intent is to do away with agencies that promote and protect DEI, as well as eliminate DEI terms from all laws and regulations (and probably books, after that). Not only do they want to eliminate support for these concepts, clearly they want to gradually remove these notions from the American consciousness.

And so back to "Christian" nationalism. The Bible addresses DEI, not in those terms, but in no uncertain terms. A key tenet of Christianity is to put others before ourselves. In the text we see "others" also referred to as "neighbors" and "strangers." Others, neighbors, and strangers, which obviously includes immigrants, constitute *diversity*. A second related principle of the faith is to treat others as you would want others to treat you. Sounds like *equity* to me. Deep equity, in fact. And third is inclusion. Diversity and equity can't exist without inclusion occurring, and the Bible's emphasis on neighbor, church family, and flock hammers home God's desire for us to be *inclusive*.

There are three additional giveaways that probably should arouse suspicion about "Christian" nationalists. First is their fear of woke and critical race theory. The Bible directs us to be humble. Those who are humble are not afraid to take a deep and honest look at themselves and self-critique. And unlike narcissists, they are able to recognize, acknowledge, and take responsibility for their, their ancestors', and their nation's shortcomings and wrongdoings.

The second is their own term for themselves. Nationalism of any kind implies exclusiveness, separation, and supremacy. And by default it means a complementary "...ism" of some kind must exist as well ... racism, ethnicism, sexism, classism. It's hard to see "putting others before ourselves" in any of those. And the Bible further confirms God's contempt for nationalism with his words on idolatry and giving allegiance to anyone or anything other than himself.

And third is their increasingly angry attempts to legislatively, judicially, and in some cases violently defend the institution of Chrisianity. But Christians know that nothing can banish God, extinguish Christianity, or prohibit them from being faithful. They are unthreatened, and they know God does not need their protection. What message are these conservatives sending if their plan is to staff their government with political appointees, twist the Constitution to serve their purpose, and then use that civic body to try to legitimize themselves and their religious identity? It's hard, right now, not to feel chilled by the specters of The Inquisition and state religion.

Critics of this last thought will say their efforts are not to mandate or impose on others their version of Christianity (yet), but to simply ensure *their personal rights* to live *their* lives according to *their* beliefs. The italicized words in this statement suggest a fourth giveaway. Christians understand that their faith is not their right or entitlement, it's a gift.

It's fair to question just how much Christianity versus how much nationalism "Christian" nationalists truly adhere to. Project 2025 makes it quite clear it's the latter. It also reveals that "Christian" nationalists have chosen to dismiss Jesus. "What you do for the least of these, you do for me" is falling on "... ears that cannot hear."

Far right conservatives have simply come up with another front for white nationalism, which, in turn, is a front for white supremacy. And that – white supremacy – is America's true deep state, not Americans who are trying to put others before themselves, or at least care for others as they hope others will care for them.

| 15 |

Will Vermont Remain Below Average? (2024)

(A Vermont-specific version of "Deep State, Indeed")

According to research conducted by the Public Religion Research Institute (PRRI) and the Brookings Institute, 30% of Americans, 40% of red states, 55% of Republicans, and 55% of those who "hold a favorable view of Trump" are likely to either adhere to or sympathize with Christian Nationalism. In contrast, just over 20% of blue states, 25% of Independents, and 16% of Democrats are likely to hold Christian Nationalist views (www.prri.org/research). Granted, this is just one study, but one that was conducted by two organizations I think most agree are reputable and nonpartisan. I'll share Vermont's numbers shortly.

The Heritage Foundation (THF), a conservative group promoting Christian Nationalism, has been making headlines lately for their manifesto titled Project 2025: Presidential Transition Project. In this agenda we see everything from mass deportation to dismantling the Constitution, eliminating regulatory and rights-protecting agencies, and giving the president authoritarian power. It's an effort to reverse any policy or legislation that sustains democracy, equal rights, equal opportunity, and regulations intended to protect *every* American.

It's also clearly an attempt to reinstitutionalize overt privilege for *certain* Americans, namely conservative whites. Most telling of this fact is their disdain for anything supporting diversity, equity, and inclusion (DEI). Their intent is to do away with agencies that promote and protect DEI, as well as eliminate DEI terms from all laws and regulations. Not only do they want to eliminate support for these concepts, clearly they want to gradually remove these notions from the American consciousness.

And so back to Christian Nationalism. The Bible addresses DEI, not in those terms, but in no uncertain terms. A key tenet of Christianity is to put others before self. In the text we see "others" also referred to as "neighbors" and "strangers." Others, neighbors, and strangers, which obviously includes immigrants, constitute *diversity*. A second related principle of the faith is to treat others as you want others to treat you. Sounds like *equity* to me. And third is inclusion. Diversity and equity can't exist without inclusion occurring, and the Bible's emphasis on neighbor, church family, and flock confirms God's desire for us to be *inclusive*.

There are three additional giveaways that should arouse suspicion about Christian Nationalists. First is their fear of "woke" and critical race theory. The Bible directs us to be humble. Those who are humble are not afraid to take an honest look at themselves. And unlike narcissists, they're able to recognize, acknowledge, and take responsibility for their, their ancestors', and their nation's shortcomings and wrongdoings.

The second is their own term for themselves. Nationalism of any kind implies exclusiveness and supremacy. And by default it means a complementary "...ism" of some kind exists as well ... racism, ethnicism, sexism, classism. It's hard to see "putting others before self" in any of those. And the Bible further confirms God's contempt for nationalism with his words on idolatry and giving allegiance to anyone or anything other than himself.

And third is their increasingly angry attempts to legislatively, judicially, and, in some cases, violently defend Christianity. But Christians tell us that nothing can banish God, extinguish Christianity, or prohibit them from being faithful. They are unthreatened, and they know God does not need their protection. What message are Christian Nationalists sending if their plan is to staff the government with political appointees, gut the Constitution to serve their purpose, and then use that civic body to try to legitimize themselves and their religious identity? It's hard, right now, not to feel chilled by the specter of state religion.

Critics of this last thought will say their efforts are not to impose on others their version of Christianity, but to simply ensure *their personal rights* to live *their* lives according to *their* beliefs. The italicized words in this statement suggest a fourth giveaway. Christians understand that their faith is not an entitlement, it's a gift, and one that's available to all.

It's fair to question just how much Christianity versus how much nationalism Christian Nationalists truly adhere to. Project 2025 makes it obvious it's the latter. It also reveals that Christian Nationalists, in their rage against DEI, are willfully dismissing Jesus's words, "What you do for the least of these, you do for me."

And so back to Vermont. 31% of Vermonters voted for Trump in 2020, and 28% either adhere to or sympathize with Christian Nationalism. The correlation PRRI shows between Republicans, Trump supporters, and Christian Nationalists is evident. On the other hand, Vermont's average score on PRRI's Christian Nationalism scale is 0.29, which is below the national average and puts Vermont solidly in the category of being "skeptical" of Christian Nationalism.

Here's to Vermont for being below average.

| 16 |

Time for Some Honest Introspection (2024)

T he final vote tally* for this year's presidential election is telling. Damning, actually.

We know that a number of prominent Republicans who previously supported Donald Trump for president publicly confirmed they would not vote for him this time. Surely, even more were privately committing, as well. And, it's likely most of us know *at least one* personal acquaintance who voted for him in 2016, but has since abandoned him. So with all of this lost support, surely he would do worse than he did in 2020, right?

He received 77.2 million votes, 3 million more than in 2020. How did he do that?

Trump supporters will respond that his increased support was because a large number of Democrats voted Republican because they feel their party has forgotten them. But was it disaffected Democrats, more turnout from his base, or both? It's intriguing trying to make sense of his numbers. But what's especially curious is that he won the election by 2.3 million votes. How did he do *that?*

A look at Kamala Harris's numbers provides a clearer picture. Not only did she receive 2.3 million less votes than Trump, curiously she received 6.3 million less votes than her predecessor, Joe Biden, who got 7 million more votes than Trump in 2020. Combine this with the fact that *3.6 million less votes were cast in this election,* and a disturbing story emerges.

So who did those Trump defectors vote for? And what about the 7 million voters who voted for Biden over Trump in 2020? Who got their votes this time? The numbers reveal these votes didn't go to Trump. He only received 77.2 (49.9%) of the 154.8 million votes cast. They didn't go to an alternative party candidate or write-in candidates, either. Combined, they only received 1.7% of the vote, the smallest percentage for that block of candidates in the last three elections.

Clearly, a large majority of these voters did not vote for Harris, with perhaps as many as 3.6 million of them being those who chose to not vote, period.

Why did those who abandoned Trump not vote for Harris? Party loyalty? But to not step up to stop someone who is promising to terminate the Constitution, even if it meant voting for someone in the opposing party? Odd, especially considering the person they allowed to win promised, in 2015, to destroy their party, and has done just that.

Other reasons we heard for not voting for Harris are just as disturbing. Some claimed they didn't know enough about her to risk voting for her. But why didn't they know enough about her? Given what they knew about Trump's misconduct, why didn't they bother to take some time to read up on her?

Others weren't sure she was qualified enough to be president. Given all they knew about Trump, wouldn't it have been worth the time to research and compare their respective (dis)qualifications? *Why did they simply dismiss her without a second look?*

Perhaps they didn't vote for her because she rubbed them the wrong way, they couldn't warm up to her, or they just don't like her. But to not vote for her, knowing it would risk putting the candidate they abandoned back in office, suggests an extraordinary level of contempt. What could they have witnessed during her mostly behind the scenes work as vice president and during her historically brief campaign that would warrant disliking her that much?

And what about the 6.3 million people who helped Biden defeat Trump but chose not to help Harris defeat Trump. Their prior vote for Biden implies they support the Democrat Party and they oppose Trump. Even if they didn't like Harris, know enough about her, or feel she wasn't qualified enough, it's highly likely they would have still voted for her, especially given that her opponent was Trump.

The elephant in the room is demanding attention. *Over 6 million more people voted for Biden when Trump was starting to show signs of being dangerous than voted for Harris as Trump was publicly announcing just exactly how dangerous he is.* What's truly behind why these voters were willing to risk a Trump win rather than vote for Harris?

By helping Trump get elected, those voters have helped advance Project 2025, a political agenda initiated by the far right that is steeped in racism, Christian nationalism, white nationalism, and misogyny. Apparently, "... far right ..." no longer applies, and that begs the question. Is it a "deep state" or "deep hate" problem we have in this country?

2016/2020 figures courtesy of www.usa.gov/votingandelections

as of 1:30 PM, December 11, 2024 courtesy of The Associated Press (www.ap.org)

| 17 |

Vermont, Gov. Scott, and Individual Rights (2025)

Two fundamental issues dividing Republicans and Democrats are taxes and spending, and the size and jurisdiction of government. There are others, and the differences between the parties can't simply be reduced to these two. But when we look closely at their policy arguments, we typically find these differing views on taxes and the role of government embedded somewhere.

But it's deeper than that. What underlies their stances on these two issues is the ultimate divide between Republicans and Democrats ... their views on the sanctity of individual rights and liberties, and specifically who "individual" refers to when it comes to those individual rights and liberties.

There are Democrats and Republicans, alike, who genuinely accept that the term "individual rights" does not simply mean "my rights," but rather "the rights every individual deserves." They sincerely want to respect, with as much deference as possible, the rights of others, no matter how much they conflict with their own.

And then there are those who believe that their rights trump the rights of others.

There's no better or more timely example of this moral dilemma than here in Vermont, and Governor Phil Scott highlighted it in his January 9, 2025 inaugural address (https://governor.vermont.gov/pressrelease/transcript). Listen closely to these excerpts from his speech.

- "... (they) trusted them (their legislators) to put the people they represent *first* ..."
- "Let's put our communities above all else and reset the playing field so it's fair and benefits all of Vermont."
- "We're not here to worry about egos. We're here to do what Vermonters need."
- "... think about what they (hard working taxpayers) can afford and what they need; and give everyone the chance to not *just* survive, but to thrive."
- "... make it (education funding) work better for all kids ..."
- "What priorities of theirs (constituents) will you (legislators) have addressed?"
- "... we keep affordability for everyone our top priority."
- "We've welcomed over 1,000 refugees in the last three years, and we will continue to do our part."
- "... Vermonters tapped into that same sense of community to once again help neighbors (during the '23 and '24 floods)."

- "This (a flood victim's concern for other victims) is the selflessness - *this* is the stubborn sense of community - that inspires me ... make the lives of all Vermonters easier."
- "... putting the needs of your neighbors ahead of your own significant challenges ..."
- "... brighter future that all Vermonters deserve."

Sadly, Governor Scott's sentiments are not those of the voters who helped Donald Trump get elected president. What we're hearing and seeing from them is a promotion of self, greed, and their own power and standing over others (e.g., racism, misogyny, white nationalism, and Christian nationalism). The Republican Party's general support of Project 2025 confirms this, as does the fact that Trump, a proponent of Project 2025, won the election. *Their allegiance to these superiority and entitlement beliefs implies that, for them, there is no moral dilemma over whose lives and rights matter more.*

Where does this self-centered mindset come from? It's not encouraged in our country's Declaration of Independence ("... all men are created equal ... endowed by their Creator with certain unalienable Rights, that among them are Life, Liberty and the pursuit of Happiness."). It's contrary to patriotism. To be a patriot means to be willing to sacrifice yourself to protect the rights and liberties of your fellow countrymen and countrywomen. It's certainly not supported by the Bible. The key tenet of Christianity is to put others before ourselves. It's not sanctioned by the Constitution. That evolving document is all about ensuring greater equality and rights for *more* Americans, not less. And it's not endorsed by the 1964 Civil Rights Act, which prohibits discrimination based on race, color, religion, sex, or national origin.

It appears that their worldview is not governed by patriotism, the Constitution, or any religion that encourages humility. Rather, it stems from their steadfast belief that competition is everything. With that comes their adherence to social Darwinism, the notions of survival of the fittest and zero sum game, and classism of all kinds. And that, I suppose, is where their need for superiority and feelings of entitlement come from, and subsequently their negativity toward taxes and government as well as their perception that they are the "individual" in individual rights.

Governor Scott is right. There are no "silver bullets" for making sure everyone's rights are respected and needs are met. I appreciate he's at least aiming for it.

| 18 |

Please Keep Up Your Good Works, Vermont (2025)

"Mass Deportation Now!" signs and "Send them back!" cheers filled the air at Donald Trump's campaign rallies. He and his supporters say their rage is over illegal immigrants, but it's hard not to question that, and here's why.

Through executive order, Trump has taken away immigration enforcement protections for safe sites such as schools, churches, and healthcare facilities. He has halted the humanitarian protection program for people trying to flee Venezuela, Haiti, Nicaragua, and Cuba. He is trying to undo birthright citizenship, guaranteed by the 14th Amendment, for children of immigrants born here. He is creating situations where whole families, including members here legally, will be forced to consider leaving to avoid being separated. He has shut down CBP One, the Customs and Border Protection Agency's app for undocumented immigrants to apply for legal entrance, and canceled already scheduled appointments. He continues to explore charging asylum seekers a fee. And he has placed federal diversity, equity, and inclusion (DEI) staff on leave.

Why is it fair to question that it's only "illegals" Trump and his followers are after? For starters, mistakes are sure to occur in a rushed and emotionally charged mass deportation effort. Border Czar, Tom Homan, admits there will be collateral arrests (CNN;1/21/24). Has Trump issued an executive order ensuring no legal immigrants end up "collaterals?"

Here are more reasons for skepticism. Hoping to pressure whole immigrant families to leave, whether U.S. citizens or not, goes beyond just "illegals." Terminating official channels for immigrants to legally enter our country does, as well. Discouraging and preventing asylum seekers from trying to legally enter the U.S. by charging them a fee isn't targeting "illegals." Combine these with simultaneously doing away with DEI staff, part of Project 2025's openly white nationalist agenda, and the goal is obvious.

Trump's Homeland Security Advisor and White House Deputy Chief of Staff for Policy, Stephen Miller, admitted it at a Trump rally at Madison Square Garden (10/28/2024) … "America is for Americans and Americans only!" Maybe he meant, "America is for Americans who are legally American and for legal Americans only!" But that's not what he said. Americans aren't stupid, they know exactly what he meant, and the 2024 election results suggest the majority of them are right there with him.

And then there's Vermont.

Perhaps Google's AI Overview service captures Vermont and immigration best. Type in "anti-immigration activists in Vermont" and you'll see the following. "There is not much information about anti-immigration activists in Vermont, but there are many immigrant rights activists and organizations in the state." Go to (https://www.findlaw.com/immigration/immigration-laws-and-resources/vermont-state-immigration-laws.html) and you'll find this quote. "This (ACLU vs. VT DMV) settlement shows that Vermont is more favorable to immigrants' rights ... Vermont is where immigrants get more protection." You'll find the following fact on the Immigrant Legal Resource Center's website (https://www.ilrc.org/state-map-immigration-enforcement-2024). In 2024, Vermont was ranked in the top ten states providing immigrant protection. And finally, from our state Agency of Human Services State Refugee Office. "The mission ... promote and provide a safe and welcoming home for refugees and immigrants, and to promote their full participation as self-sufficient individuals and families in the economic, social, and civic life of Vermont."

Combine these with the fact that two thirds of Vermont voters rejected Trump and his anti-immigrant proposals, and it's easy to see where Vermont stands on immigration. *Yet, one third of Vermont voters did cast their vote directly for Trump.*

In recent decades, immigrants have never comprised more than 5% of Vermont's population, and only once reached 6% of its workforce.* Maybe those voters picked Trump out of concern for our nation as a whole. As recently as 2022, immigrants made up 18% of the nation's total workforce (https://www.pewresearch.org/short-reads/2024/09/27/key-findings-about-us-immigrants/). In 2023, they were 14.3% of its total population (https://usafacts.org/answers/how-many-immigrants-are-in-the-us/state/vermont/). Do these numbers justify the kind of mass deportation effort Trump is commanding?

Christian nationalists are a driving force behind America's war on immigration, despite what the Bible says about nationalism and entitlement, the two beliefs central to anti-immigrant sentiment. It denounces nationalism of any kind, and reminds us that *all* belongs to God. It's hard not to assume "all" includes America and "American" jobs.

So why did that third of voters help re-elect Trump? Yes, inflation was part of his platform. But given his disproportionate focus on demonizing immigrants, *which voters could not have missed*, it's a fair guess they chose him for that, too. Because if they felt Christian love, or even just indifference, toward immigrants, there's no way they would then turn and scapegoat them simply in hopes of cheaper eggs.

*　(https://www.migrationpolicy.org/data/state-profiles/state/demographics/VT)

(https://www.americanimmigrationcouncil.org/sites/default/files/research/immigrants_in_vermont.pdf)

| 19 |

Are We Better Off Now Than Nine Years Ago? (2025)

The following three commentaries were written back in 2016-17. Nothing was made of them at the time but I decided I'd hold on to them anyway. Then just the other day something prompted me to look at them again. Are you as alarmed as I am that they're just as relevant today as they were back then? Talk about one step forward, two steps backwards.

SAD! (2016)

Racists, bigots, xenophobes, supremacists, and national- ists are nothing new. They've been around and dividing our country since its beginning. What *is* new is a president (and his administration and Cabinet) who seems to empathize with all of them and openly sympathizes with one in particular, white nationalists.

White nationalists believe white Americans are losing their standing in society. They are especially irked that, in their minds, their demise is at the hands of non-whites and "non-Americans." Blacks are climbing America's career ladders, Hispanics are undercutting American workers and stealing their blue collar jobs, Jews are accumulating more than their fair share of America's wealth, and New Americans are taking over America's top white collar jobs.

Ironically, blacks, Hispanics, Jews, and New Americans are not the problem. They're simply participating in capitalism. The problem is capitalism, itself, and its inability to prevent unequal accumulation of wealth and truly provide equal economic opportunity for *all.*

Rather than hating and fighting to change the economic system that is failing them, white nationalists instead choose to hate and fight those who happen to be doing relatively well for now in that system … just as they were when it was their turn to do so.

Hypocrisy (2016)

It would be ignorant and irresponsible to lump together the alt right, neo-Nazis, Republicans, white nationalists, Libertarians, white supremacists, the Tea Party, and others of the conservative right as one and the same. However, what they have in common is a bit alarming.

For one, they're all parties of fear and anger. Each fears losing what they believe gives them power and standing in society, and they're angry at groups who they perceive are the beneficiaries of their loss. Consequently, their political bottom lines are the same ... protecting their self-interests over the interests of others. Trump and his administration, sycophants, and surrogates fit this bill perfectly. They'll argue they're out for what's best for our country but it's difficult to find anything they're proposing and fighting for that doesn't ultimately boil down to selfish gain, self-protection, self-preservation, and self-centeredness.

There's a second, rather contradictory commonality among right wing groups. Their subscribers generally claim to belong to the Christian church. If so, then what's with all the fear and hate, and why aren't they humbly viewing others above themselves and putting others' needs ahead of their own?

True Patriots (2017)

The growing number of professional athletes and others kneeling during our national anthem is causing outrage. Those offended say these people are unpatriotic and their actions are a slap in the face to our men and women who defend our flag. Those who side with the protesters say they are simply exercising their First Amendment right to free speech. Who's correct?

The answer comes down to which defines our country ... our flag, or our Constitution?

Unlike the flag, the Constitution literally defines America. And embedded in that definition is the guaranteed right of every American to freely and without fear of reprisal express their beliefs and concerns. It makes sense, then, that our true patriots are those who live by and defend our Constitution. By honoring our Constitution they honor our country.

And our flag? It's no small hypocrisy that some of our most ardent defenders of allegiance to our flag are divisive white nationalists who pay greater homage to the Confederate flag than the U. S. flag, and states' rights advocates who essentially want less national unity, not more. These people are quick to cry out to the protesters, "Love it (the *United* States) or leave it!" Again, the hypocrisy is astonishing. Their fake allegiance to our flag, frustration with free speech, and disdain for the protesters clearly reveal they don't love our country.

And finally, shame on those who are using our military and veterans as cover to hide the real reason they hate those who are kneeling. Our military does not defend our flag. The image of our troops encircling every flagpole in our country 24/7 is comical. Our military defends our country, which means they defend our Constitution. And that means they are defending our right to kneel during the national anthem.

| 20 |

Who's Right, and Who's Out in Left Field? (2025)

Years ago, while working for an environmental education organization, we created what we called an "ecological filter." It was a checklist for use by anyone planning a habitat project (planting trees, removing a hedge, etc.) to assess how eco-friendly their plan was. For example, one criterion was, "Will this project, at a minimum, sustain your current level of local biodiversity?"

The two "filters" I'm using here are universal. They're found in a number of different religions, but if you don't subscribe to any religion, no worries. We learned them both in kindergarten. For a fun read, check out Robert Fulghum's book, *All I Really Need to Know I learned in Kindergarten*, published in 1986.

The two "filters" are the golden rule (treat others as you wish others to treat you) and putting others' needs and interests ahead of our own.

But first, some background. We know every action has a ripple effect, direct and indirect results, and is beneficial or detrimental depending on who's impacted. Take this simplified example of shoplifting. The ripple effect extends from store owners losing money, to having to spend money for security, having to raise prices to make up for that, which hurts other customers, causing store owners to lose customers, which impacts the local economy, and so on. A direct effect is money lost on items stolen. An indirect effect is any byproduct from the stress of guarding against theft. The benefit for shoplifters is the satisfaction of some material or emotional need, but the loss of income is detrimental to the store owners.

Thinking ecologically like this helps us answer questions such as, "If I choose to (fill in the blank), am I honoring the golden rule and considering others first?"

The following are common issues dividing the left (liberals, progressives, Democrats) and right (conservatives, Republicans, Libertarians). Where do the left and right *generally* stand on these issues, and how do their stances measure up against these two criteria? I emphasize "generally" because one-size-doesn't-fit-all.

First up, immigration. Given the results of the 2024 election, it's safe to say that, generally, the right wants to allow fewer legal immigrants, refugees, and asylum seekers into our country than the left is open to. Which stance seems more in line with our two "filters?"

And what about the following stances?

Project 2025. As evidenced by its embeddedness in his executive orders (ex. eliminating DEI), the number of Project 2025 people he's slipping into his administration (ex. Russ Vought, Office of Management and Budget), and items in the agenda he's already implementing (exs. freezing federal funding and dismantling government agencies), Trump supports it. Logic suggests his conservative supporters do, too. The left, on the other hand, generally opposes its support of racism, misogyny, white nationalism, Christian nationalism, and authoritarian power.

Related to Project 2025 is diversity, equity, and inclusion (DEI). Trump, his administration, and political leaders elected on the right are trying to eliminate DEI. Elected leaders on the left are fighting to keep it alive.

Gun control is divisive, as well. The right is generally more opposed to restrictions on gun ownership than the left. They argue the Second Amendment guarantees their right to purchase, own, and legally use a gun. The left doesn't disagree, but generally argues that because of growing criminal use of guns, and the escalating number of innocent victims of gun violence, tighter purchase and ownership restrictions and prohibitions are needed.

Climate change is contentious, too. The left generally expresses alarm that there's a climate crisis, and the right generally downplays it. And then there's the rub over how to respond to it, if at all. The left wants tougher environmental protections, government mandated if necessary. The right doesn't want the government stepping in and imposing "unreasonable" costs on businesses. If there actually is a crisis, they want free market-driven ingenuity to solve it ... the very drive that created it.

And then there's taxation. Generally, the right and the left agree there's a need for taxation. They differ over how much, for what, and who should benefit. The right argues for less taxation. Trickle-down economics and charitable giving will suffice. The left recognizes that capitalism and generosity don't adequately assist the poor, and Christians tell us it's a must that we do (Mark 14:7; Deuteronomy 15:7-11; et. al.). Yet the problem persists, and so that's why government intervention is necessary.

With respect to the golden rule and putting others first, who's right and who's out in left field? If we truly want to answer the question honestly, it's important we look at the ripple, direct/indirect, and cost/benefit effects of each party's stance. Or, we can do the simple thing, leave our blinders on, and just stick to our legacy biases.

| 21 |

Civil War? (2025)

As far back as 2017, we heard cries for civil war from President Trump's base. Alex Jones of Infowars.com, a prominent Trump follower, argued it was necessary. (https://www.newsweek.com/trump-alex-jones-infowars-violence-639912) Michael Savage, host of "The Savage Nation" talk show threatened, "... there's going to be a civil war ..."(ibid) On January 6, 2021, there was a conservative led insurrection on our nation's Capitol Building. Since then, Jones has been praised by Republican Vice President J. D. Vance. (https://www.propublica.org/article/jd-vance-alex-jones-leonard-leo-teneo-maddow) And today, we don't even need the dark web anymore to see who's promoting that same level of violence. (https://www.journalofdemocracy.org/articles/the-rise-of-political-violence-in-the-united-states/) Is civil war imminent?

First, a word about "civil war." Is a civil war solely a prolonged armed conflict between states or nations, as it's typically defined? According to the Merriam-Webster dictionary, "civil" means of, relating to, or consisting of states or citizens, and "war" is a state of prolonged hostility, conflict, or antagonism. Those definitions suggest a "civil war" can be a conflict between nations or individuals, and not necessarily an armed one. So if two reliably informed (or not) individuals go at it non-violently over things related to state and/or citizenry (i.e., politics), is that a civil war?

Arguably it is, especially considering that what we typically remember most about our Civil War (1861-1865) was how it pitted neighbors, friends, and family members against each other, first morally, then violently.

In his 2023 book, *"The Undertow: Scenes from a Slow Civil War,"* Vermont author Jeff Sharlet describes what he calls "slow civil war." He talks of the various ideologies that are fueling our culture war and slowly expanding the divide in our country. Examples include white supremacy and racism, conspiracy theory, Christian privilege and prosperity gospel, and spiritual warfare and end times ideology. Fortunately, this "slow civil war" among our citizenry has been just that. A gradual tribalism of hearts and minds, slowly escalating mostly as a war of words, not bullets. But not that slowly. How many of us know of, or perhaps are part of, a neighbor, friend, or family civil war right now? I'm in the midst of one, myself.

Americans are divided over democracy as defined by the Declaration of Independence, Constitution, Bill of Rights, and 1964 Civil Rights Act, as well as implied in the golden rule. Do we want that version of democracy, or something else?

In this past election we had a choice for president. We could vote for Trump, who was out to end democracy, or

Kamala Harris, who promised to preserve democracy. Do you know someone who, despite knowing Trump's plans, voted for him anyway? How about someone who had abandoned Trump after his first term yet still chose not to vote for Harris, knowingly taking a chance Trump could win?

Regarding the latter, why would someone take that risk? Party loyalty? But to not step up to stop someone who promised to terminate the Constitution, even if it meant voting for someone in the opposing party? Odd, especially considering the person they helped to win had previously promised to destroy their beloved party. (https://www.cnn.com/2016/10/11/politics/donald-trump-campaign-republican-party/index.html)

Perhaps they felt they didn't know enough about her to risk voting for her. But why didn't they know enough about her? Given what they knew about Trump at that point, why didn't they bother to take some time to read up on her?

Maybe they didn't feel she was qualified enough to be president. Again, wouldn't it have been worth the time to research and compare their respective (dis)qualifications? *Why did they simply dismiss her without a second look?*

Or was it simply because they just don't like her. But to not vote for her, knowing it could mean a Trump victory, suggests an extraordinary level of contempt. What could they possibly have witnessed during her mostly behind the scenes work as vice president or during her historically brief campaign that would warrant disliking her that much?

The elephant in the room is demanding attention. What *is* behind why someone would risk a Trump win rather than vote for Harris? Incidentally (coincidentally?), by enabling

Trump to get elected they helped advance Project 2025, an agenda initiated by conservatives that promotes and is fueled by racism, Christian nationalism, white nationalism, misogyny, and authoritarianism.

And now you know my civil war. I suspect some readers are appalled that someone would be so disloyal as to put politics ahead of neighbor, friend, or family member. Others, I believe, understand it's deeper than that. Who *are* we here for? Who *should* we be here for? This is more than simply a political divide, it's a moral dilemma.

| 22 |

Separate But Equal Silos?
(2025)

One notable advocate for making sure a democracy's citizenry is informed was Thomas Jefferson. He knew that for a democratic nation to thrive, its citizens need to understand the issues impacting society and government. They also need to know their rights and responsibilities, the history of their country, and how their government works. To ensure a nation's citizenry is sufficiently informed, he believed public education is key. (The Role of Education | Thomas Jefferson's Monticello)

Horace Mann, of Massachusetts, helped public education become even more public through his Common School movement in the mid-1800's. (PBS: Only A Teacher: Horace Mann (1796-1859)). America was starting to move away from schools that focused on teaching Latin or just the "3 R's", or were only open to boys, whites, or those who could afford to attend. And then with Brown vs. Board of Education (1954), and the desegregation of public schools, it ap-

peared America finally had a true public education system ...
on paper, anyway.

After more than 300 years of striving toward a knowl-
edgeable citizenry, you would think we'd have one. Today,
we not only have public education (for now, anyway), but
thanks to technology we have more access to more available
information than ever before. Sadly, that technology and access aren't equally available to all Americans, but compared
to back in the day, surely a greater percentage of us are now
able to be informed than at any other time in our history ...
if we so choose.

Jefferson's concern over not having an "informed citizenry" and its risk to democracy is appearing prophetic. But
is what's happening to our country the result of us being uninformed? Or is it because we are selectively informed, and
therefore potentially misinformed?

The term I use below, "news silos," refers to in-depth lib-
eral- and conservative-leaning news sources.

We know, from cognitive science, about attention span,
ability to retain information, construction of knowledge,
and cognitive dissonance. For more on these, start with
research written about by Renate and Geoff Caine. Given
our human limitations in these areas, it's understandable
why we gravitate to news silos. They provide a neater, sim-
pler, and more comfortable way for us to construct understanding. To survive information overload we become
selective and tend to generalize and compartmentalize. And
in the process, our silo becomes a source of confirmation
and affirmation, which feel much better than ambiguity and

dissonance. Like silage, our knowledge and understanding become the cured product of our chosen news silo.

An example of being in a news silo is one's decision to watch just CNN or FOX News. Consuming our news only from Breitbart News, FOX News, and the National Review, or from Democracy Now, CNN, and The Atlantic, are examples, as well.

So is where we are politically in this country simply because of ignorance? Or because our news silos are, in fact, separate but *not* equal? No doubt, there are citizens among us who are truly uninformed through no fault of their own. There are others who willingly stay uninformed. And still others, willfully. My focus here is on the willfully uninformed.

First, a thought on silos. The cylindrical structure agricultural enterprises use to store feed and forage is now a metaphor for how we generally consume news. "Bubble" is another. Our nation has become so divided politically, it seems that healthy discourse is gone forever. And rather than peek into others' silos, open to being persuaded or humbly willing to see if perhaps we're wrong, we instead simply turn away from them, often hatefully.

Again, there are reasons why we tend toward news silos. And by patronizing a news silo we claim we are informed. But if our information is insular and compartmentalized, then is our understanding valid? *If we choose to only take in news from within a biased silo, are we not willfully choosing to be ignorant?*

It's totally understandable if we feel a need to silo because of information overload, news devolving into soundbites, feeling there are so few, if any, sources we can trust any-more, or for lack of anywhere to go to have a civil political debate. And if we choose to silo because our worldview is set in stone, well, that's understandable, too … but in a different and not so generous sense.

If news silos (i.e., willful ignorance) are the future, I hope we'll at least commit to regularly asking ourselves the following question. When I'm done taking in my news for the day, do I find myself thinking simply about how what's going on will affect me, or how it's also going to impact every other person in my community and society at large?

| 23 |

Why Republicans and Not Democrats? (2025)

Socio-political forces that had been mostly behind the scenes are now front and center. Why is that? Why have these forces, by and large, aligned themselves with the Republican Party? And why are they channeling their efforts through congressional Republicans, rather than Democrats?

The forces I'm referring to include right wing extremist groups, white nationalists, white supremacists, misogynists, anti-constitutionalists, oligarch wannabes, and Vladimir Putin sympathizers.

QAnon is one of those right wing extremist groups. They believe our country is led by evildoers controlled by Satan. In their quest to be heard they attached themselves to the Republican Party and Donald Trump, who they view as their savior. (https://www.prri.org/research/the-persistence-of-qanon-in-the-post-trump-era-an-analysis-of-who-believes-the-conspiracies/) What is it about the

Republican Party that QAnon members feel connected with?

White nationalists believe that our nation was, is, and needs to remain white. They fear and hate that people of color are "replacing" them. The politically conservative Heritage Foundation has produced Project 2025, a conservative agenda that responds to and promotes this fear and hatred. Trump has inserted hundreds of Project 2025 contributors into his Republican administration, many of whom were officials in his first administration. (https://www.afge.org/article/new-trump-administration-packed-with-project-2025-architects/) Why do white nationalists feel solidarity with the Republican Party?

"There were good people on both sides!" Trump's thumbs up to white supremacists after the August 12, 2017 "Unite the Right" neo-Nazi march in Charlottesville, Virginia, was just additional confirmation for them that they had picked the right party to align themselves with. But that "marriage" didn't begin with Trump. It's existed since at least the 1950's. (https://www.motherjones.com/politics/2022/09/it-didnt-start-with-trump-the-decades-long-saga-of-how-the-gop-went-crazy/) Why do white supremacists feel a sense of belonging with the Republican Party?

When it comes to misogyny and Republican Party leadership, look no further than the Oval Office. (https://www.usatoday.com/story/opinion/columnist/2024/08/14/trump-sexist-vance-republican-misogyny-women/74631430007/) This relationship didn't start with the emergence of Trump, either. History suggests it began in the 1800's when the Republican Party shifted their advocacy from women to southern white voters angry over integration legislation. Their deprioritization of women came to a head in 1980 when the GOP turned its focus away from the Equal Rights Amendment. (https://psmag.com/news/when-the-republican-party-stopped-endorsing-feminism/) What is it about the Republican Party that allows outspoken proponents of misogyny to feel empowered?

What about anti-constitutionalists? Today's Republican Party is abandoning Jeffersonian Republicanism, and the Constitution as we know it, and moving toward something more Federalist (for the moment). (https://www.pbs.org/wgbh/americanexperience/features/duel-federalist-and-republican-party/) It wants to suppress civil and human rights, as well as undo diversity, equity, and inclusion (DEI) efforts. And it wants a more authoritarian executive branch. Why do anti-constitutionalists feel affiliation with the Republican Party?

Oligarch wannabes fit this bill, as well. Rather than try to do justice here, I encourage you to read Ari Berman's 2024 book, *Minority Rule: The Right-Wing Attack on the Will of the People – and the Fight to Resist It*, for an in-depth look at America's relationship with oligarchy.

And finally, Putin sympathizers. Trump is an outspoken admirer and defender of Vladimir Putin. Former Republican representative, now Director of National Intelligence, Tulsi Gabbard has revealed she is, too. To go along with this, Trump (with consent from the Republican majority Senate), as he did with Gabbard, has appointed unqualified and mostly inexperienced Republicans such as former FOX

News host Pete Hegseth (Secretary of Defense), former representative Michael Waltz (National Security Advisor), former governor Kristi Noem (Secretary of Homeland Security), and attorneys Kash Patel (FBI Director) and Pam Bondi (Attorney General) to head the very agencies that protect us from domestic and foreign threats … like Russia. Their charge is to streamline (gut and then dismantle?) their respective agencies. (no citations needed for these widely substantiated facts)

Are Trump and the Republican Party methodically weakening our country's defense? Are they doing it on purpose? That's crazy, you say? I hope you're right.

What's not crazy is the fact that each of these groups, Trump as well, is a threat to democracy, and all have aligned themselves with the Republican Party. Why Republicans and not Democrats?

Please note: Nowhere in this piece do I state that these groups and "ordinary, everyday" Republicans are one and the same. I am simply curious, as I hope you are, why people with these allegiances feel so at home with the Republican Party.

AFTERWORD

As you read these commentaries, I'm sure you noticed a focus on hypocrisy. We're all hypocritical at times. What's important, though, is to at least recognize and acknowledge when we're being a hypocrite, and make amends accordingly.

Trump, MAGA, and Project 2025 conservatives accuse liberals and progressives of engaging in "cancel culture" and trying to erase our history. Taking down confederate flags, dishonoring known racists and misogynists by taking away their statues and removing their names from public property, gun control efforts, and health officials pointing out the harmful effects of eating red meat are all viewed as an assault on American heritage. These are just a handful of examples. An additional grievance of theirs that is particularly alarming is their hateful assault on woke and critical race theory. Their purported reason? It will cause children to feel guilty and "teach" people to hate America. The real reason? It will expose ugly truths about us as individuals, our ancestors, and our nation ... something narcissists and supremacists can't bear.

And so back to hypocrisy. The way these conservatives are attempting to combat this attack on American heritage is to – you guessed it – attack American heritage. They are attempting to erase our constitutional heritage by methodically terminating the Constitution. Whitewashing our proud history of patriots and patriotism is part of their methodology, as well. One example is their attempt to redefine patriotism by honoring the January 6 insurrectionists while at the same time demonizing those who are trying to save our democracy and uphold the rule of law. And, they are trying to cancel the Christian heritage our nation was founded on by distorting Christian doctrine in a way that supports racism, misogyny, and white nationalism. Hence the title and cover photo of this book

The culmination of all of that is just too astonishing not to point out. The Revolutionary War was fought by our ancestors so that our nation would no longer be ruled by a king/monarchy ("dictator"), but would instead be a democracy. Conservatives are now fighting to end democracy and anoint an autocratic dictator ("king"). Talk about erasing and/or canceling culture. The hypocrisy is truly stunning.

Unless, of course, it isn't hypocrisy at all, but something even more nefarious.

ADDENDUM

I want to express my gratitude to The Times Argus (Barre, VT), The Caledonian Record (St. Johnsbury, VT), and VT-Digger (Montpelier, VT) for their willingness over the past eight years to publish some of these commentaries, and their willingness to give "the little guy" a chance to have their say. I hope these commentaries were constructive contributions.

Repeal and E'race' (VTDigger, 11/23/2017)

Conservatives Really Aren't (VTDigger, 12/07/2017)

Separating Religion and Politics? (VTDigger, 04/09/2018)

Are Conservatives America's True Patriots? (VTDigger, 09/20/2018)

(under the title *"How Can Conservatives be America's True Patriots?"*)

Socialist Conservatives (VTDigger, 03/06/2019)

(under the title *"The Irony of Conservatives"*)

Constitutionalist, Please Step Up (VTDigger, 05/09/2019)

Make America Good (The Times Argus, 01/18/2020)

Unmasking the Right (The Times Argus, 07/28/2020)

Dichotomy, Hypocrisy, and Humility (VTDigger, 11/22/2023)

Will Vermont Remain Below Average? (The Times Argus, 09/04/2024)

Deep State, Indeed (The Caledonian Record, 08/08/2024)

Time for Some Honest Introspection (The Caledonian Record, 12/03/2024)

Vermont, Governor Scott, and Individual Rights (The Caledonian Record, 01/17/2025;

The Times Argus, 01/18/2025)

Please Keep Up Your Good Works, Vermont (The Caledonian Record, 01/29/2025;

The Times Argus, 01/30/2015; VTDigger, 02/02/2025)

Who's Right, and Who's Out in Left Field? (The Times Argus, 02/15/2025; The Caledonian Record, 02/10/2025)

Civil War? (The Caledonian Record, 03/22/2025)

(under the title, *"Civil War? In Vermont?"*

Separate But Equal Silos? (The Caledonian Record, 04/05/2025; The Times Argus, 04/14/2025)

Why Republicans and Not Democrats? (The Caledonian Record, 04/25/2025; The Times Argus, 05/30/2025)

ACKNOWLEDGEMENTS

At this point in my life my list of acknowledgements is endless. And so I'll simply highlight those who were highly influential in my life relative to the following orientations that have shaped my worldview. Thank you so much, the rest of you. I am truly grateful.

Ecology

First and foremost, I thank my mother, Shirley Miriam Lenhart Skelding. She moved my two brothers and me to rural Pennsylvania when I was young. There I spent countless hours roaming fields, hiking through woods, and wading and fishing our local creek. She gave me the opportunity to explore, learn about, and fall in love with nature. I also thank Dr. M. Keith Kennedy, Professor of Entomology at Michigan State University, and Douglas Chapman, Executive Director of Dow Gardens in Midland, Michigan for my position as an entomologist. Being able to combine my horticulture background (thank you Delaware Valley College and Pennsylvania State University) with entomology launched my obsession with ecology. And, I am very grateful to Joseph Kiefer and Martin Kemple. They hired me to be their non-profit environmental education organization's Ecological Literacy Director. There I was able to do a deep study of ecology along with further developing my own ecological ethic.

Christianity

Again, I have my mother to thank for planting the seed by forcing us to go with her to our neighborhood Lutheran Church every Sunday. But it was Pastor Don Galardi, pastor of Community Evangelical Presbyterian Church in Owosso, Michigan, and his wife, Diedre, who helped me see what Christianity was truly about ... even if they never were able to get me to accept the Calvinist view of faith.

Critical Social Theory

It's a challenge to pinpoint one or two people for this one. I know I latched on to this orientation very early in life. Was it simply the times I grew up in ... civil rights protests, the Vietnam War, Cuban Missile Crisis, Watergate, pollution and environmental exploitation and degradation, four political assassinations, race riots, and hippies? Was it Robin Hood, who I fell in love with at a very young age? Perhaps it was my sixth grade teacher when she labeled me a rebel. One entity I am able to specify was the St. Michael's College (Colchester, VT) Graduate Education faculty, led at the time by Dr. Aostre Johnson, where I earned my Master's Degree in Education. That experience fine tuned and shored up my adherence to critical social theory, as well as the following orientations.

Phenomenology, Constructivism, and Holism

My interest in relativism most likely emerged out of my struggle with organized religion. I often refer to myself as a recovering member of "The Church of Present Day Hypocrites." The heavy emphasis of absolutes in church doctine combined with the hypocrisy of far too many churchgoers was very disillusioning. Postmodern thought became attractive to me. The deep ecology movement, Arne Naess and Fritjof Capra in particular, captured my attention. So did constructivism thanks to constructivist educators such as Jean Piaget and John Dewey. There were phenomenology theorists such as Martin Heidegger. There was also holism theory with Eugene Odum and Lynn Margulis, two of its leading theorists. The list for this section is truly endless. In-depth lists of those who influenced me in all of these areas can be found in my other two books (see "About the Author").

I am also deeply grateful to Rachel Fisher, Print and Production Director, Onion River Press, Burlington, Vermont, for her patience, superb professionalism, and assistance in making this book a reality.

And last, but not least, my wife, Linda. Thank you for all your loving support and understanding during all that time I spent hidden away writing.

Mark Skelding is a retired educator and horticulturist. He is the author of *Does Nature Approve? A Contemplation of Lawn Care Practices* (Onion River Press, 2020), which encourages readers to consider how well their approaches to gardening and lawn care align with what ecologists have revealed about nature. He is also the author of *Are We Still Grading Students?* (Onion River Press, 2021), which challenges readers to look critically at how we grade students and why. Mark is a passionate fly fisherman and gardener. He has lived in Vermont since 1985.

Mark Skelding at his alma mater, Delaware Valley University (Delaware Valley College of Science and Agriculture back when he attended) during Homecoming, 2022.